STONES
for WORDS

A Collection of Poetry
SARA M. ROBINSON

Poem –"High Strikes" first appeared in the
2013 Blue Ridge Anthology

Poem –"Small Hotel by a Sea" was awarded
2nd Prize in the 2013 Brodie Herndon Memorial
(Poetry Society of Virginia 90th anniversary celebration)

Cedar Creek Publishing
A Virginia Publisher of Virginia Books
Bremo Bluff, VA 23022
www.cedarcreekauthors.com

Printed in the United States of America

Library of Congress Control Number 2014931124

ISBN 978-0-9891465-3-1

For Carolyn

"And stone on stone is tooth for grinding raw."
– **From Maxine Kumin's poem, "Grace"**

"You compensate me, Stones."
– **From Marianne Moore's poem, "Flints, not Flowers"**

"Leave no stone unturned."
– **Unknown**

"Like a rolling stone…"
– **Bob Dylan**

"And the stones ceased their talking, rested in rows,
formed bridges and filled voids with their
shapes, small, large, smooth, and rough."
– **J. Hollifield Burton**

TABLE *of* CONTENTS

Why I Drink

Just This Once

How I Will Begin

A Mortal Writes of Immortalities

Do you think
someday someone
will discover a
wad of my poems
stuffed in the neck
of my favorite
scotch bottle?

Will the discovery
be unique in that
someone was searching
for my "missing poems"?

Or will the discoverer
be left to wonder why I
chose those particular
poems, or why, at some
moment I stopped
writing and decided
I was thirsty.

An Atheist Prays for a Word

This newfound devotion to poetry—
is this commitment to writing, placing
words just at the right marker.
A selected uni-ball pen kneels
before an altar of holy words
prepared to take the sacraments.

Lines stick out their tongues
like devout worshippers eager
to receive and eager to please.

But make no excuse for me—
my devotion is not to the priest,
it is to the mourner.
O, how I grieve for this.

Tablets will not appear for me
with words so sacrosanct
they cannot be touched.
My words will come from
the simple, the lowly amoeba
with its formless mass begging

for a shape to call its own,
and a skin that allows bits
to come in and go out.
This devotion, something that
cries for form, means
I will hear it before I see it.

              Before I write it.

A Person of Significance

As if I could figure out
just what defines me
or who I am

to do one thing or something
that sets me apart

to think of one act
or a thought that is so
good that you would notice

you would say I'm
the champ of the world

  like in a song sung by
  someone with only one name

you would ask about
    my next steps
    my next moves
something great

    like finding planets
    denting concrete
    forging irons

all these things you would
ask while we watched
our sleeping dogs
dream with twitching legs
while we wondered
what I would
do next

The Nobility of Poetry

Red blood flows
to a sea
but slowly
our hands
touch it and
it won't wash off

the nobility of poetry
lies in its ability
to state great truths
in a very very small space

to create an intimacy
with no pretense of
width or depth
height or time

an awareness
of the space itself
is to grant leave
for reverence of
this space with
its own dimension

the syllables
and strokes applied
will tell us everything
we need to know

O, the mastery of verse
clothed in satin phrases
it slips out from creases
        like an asp in hiding
to find its mark

Stones for Words

I write poetry all night long
in my sleep.   It goes on and on.
While I'm writing
I cannot stop.   So
I'll smile as you dream and

hope I find
the exact word
that will catch
on fire and burn

the pages so
when anyone touches
the lines she will shout
out: *O, she burns.*

Just like when I
read Lowell or Rich,
I'll find whoever
sleeps with stones knows
to either move them
or turn over.

Round   or   rough
Hard   or   smooth
    They either work
                for you as flint
                    fit in your worrying hand
                            or get tossed.

Feeling Up a Poem

I hate a poem
that makes me
feel like I'm
just a poor old
writer of nothing.

Is it my grammar
        or perhaps my syntax?
Maybe I'm just not
knocked around enough
        for it
to get me worked up,
        or is it worked over?

To appreciate the
finer points of
being in rhyme
or sensing the perfect meter,
I need something
I can own but
that everyone buys.

When I'm standing
next to my ambitions
do I feel them

rise to the cause?
Or am I missing
the point of it all:

                A perfect disappearance.

An Acute Sense of My Own Darkness

I don't see my fingers in the same way
when they move up and down a page

it's not like when I was a kid
and used my fingers to paint

I reach for something finer
fingertips as fountain pens
but not so big anymore

my fingers have found
tints slier than words
hidden in lines   I can feel

still the words are darker
not like the bright colors
of my youth

hues of overripe fruit
close to rot
but not quite

Pieces of String Too Short to Save

A top row of single malt scotches at Hamilton's
Mussels in garlic-butter sauce with toast
Arriving too early at the Jefferson
Old time mountain bluegrass music
I am a mountain creature's child
Allison Krause coming in over the speakers
I'm hurting and it's all because of you
A little Texas two-step between the seat rows
We talk about the seating and our old hips
Some guitar or mandolin picking behind
A lazy haze of martini mellow

Settling in to hear some good lyrics
Set to music that streams through
My consciousness and causes me
To wonder about a theory that
Purports to hold all this together

Circling Inside My Lines

You see me
building my lines
curved into a circle
driven forward by
mechanical parts
pulling and pushing
this Ferris wheel
going up and over
in a vertical circle
where you breathe in
(on the way up)
gasp for breath
(at the top)
then an exhalation
(on the way down)

And then you
can't wait to
repeat it, again!
Again! Again!
You tell the operator
that you don't
want to stop
    Don't let anyone on!
    Don't let anyone off!

You look down
on the crowds
from your seat
(vinyl held together by duct tape)
you don't look
at the rivets or bolts
you hear all
the creaks as

you head again
up to the top
    your eyes get big
    your knuckles turn white
(as you grip the restraining bar)

There's old gum
under the side rails
you search the midway
for anyone who might
see you and hold up
an arm   a signal

But you don't see anything
you can grab on to
and as you pass
the top and enter
the descent you hold
your breath
        your hands relax
        you close your eyes

The wheel slows down
and soon will stop
all this—every little part
you'll go through
a zillion times
while you wait
in this line
that begins every
line you've ever known
before you get
to the operator
and give him
your soggy ticket

Small Hotel by a Sea

If I checked into a small
boutique hotel and they
offered me a manual typewriter
what would I write?
    Notes on a scandal?
    Scuffmarks made by a passer-by?

Where would this hotel be?
By the ocean or on an island
in the middle of Lake Superior?
Would I try to compose lyrics
for a band called Stinkbreath or
write poetry about desperate
intersections of people with badly
fitted wigs and smelling of
dumpster diving?

Or maybe I would write a
letter to Robin and Linda Williams
telling them I don't have long
to live and would they please do
a Mavis and Marvin Smiley sketch
and sing the bluegrass version
of "Danny Boy."

Or I could write about a
couple of sixty-somethings
skateboarding in Darden Towe Park
wearing UVA beanies and lots of
protective gear not concerned about
breaking an arm or scraping a knee
but gasping at the thrill of jumping
off a ramp and landing perfectly straight.

Or I could write about picking
up orange newts (after days of rain) by
their tails and placing them on my forearm
where our eyes meet and then
I set the pulsing dotted bodies in the
wet grass begging them not to come back on
the road–their destiny to grow
bigger and turn green–I don't want
to think about their fate.

Or would I just look out the window
in my small boutique hotel and write
a line about sunset on the sea
with its yellows, blues, and reds
landscaped with silhouettes
of people simply watching–
                    waiting for the green flash.

"Take this snow-covered stone, little girl,
and make something pretty with it."
– Anonymous, circa 1954

What I Tell You

Commotio Cordis

A story revealed itself
in the last two minutes
when I found myself
paying attention–
Something about two women
one dying, one grieving
then it hit me what
the story
was all about

When I think of you
and I think of death
I'm more afraid
than you are

You say you don't want
prolonged suffering
that's your fear
I don't want to die   period
that's my fear

We face our getting older
not so happily
but with resolve
and still a spark
of that romance
we know we have

Just so you know
I still get a high blood pressure
this gasping sense
this race this stop
this shudder
when you call my name

High Strikes

This passing storm
spent of sparks
flashed its last
through the curtains
and shouted us awake

A tempestuous end
to our frantic lovemaking
leaving us to
dwell on last kisses

Muted shouts and
murmurs from us
or the storm
revealed either its
distance or
our drifting away

As rain came
down in torrents
or drizzles
we watched through
the curtains
trees caught up

in such furious
wind that we feared
all would topple
and we clung
tighter to the bed
and each other

Each jolt bound
us closer and
we marveled
we survived
both furies

Last Night You Asked Why I Write Poetry

Before I tell you—
please remove your blouse
your skin is like golden
silk laying smooth and dark
            just before sunrise

I hesitate to start—
please remove your rings
your fingers so soft
their shape so straight
            as I pause over each one

I must think of
words to describe
how poetry works for me

But before I do—
please remove your shoes
your feet and toes
so perfect and warm
the very ones that touch
me in our bed
            in our sleep

Now I can tell you—
why I write these poems
it's because I think of you
and writing is simply
            my distraction

Pour Invoquer Le Poème

When you touch the pages
where I've written my words
do you feel a difference
are there rises and falls
or crests and valleys
perhaps a peak or plateau

Can my words caress your
fingers as they mark
your progress within
the strokes and turns

If you put a page next
to your cheek
do the fine hairs
there vibrate in waves
coming out to reach you

When you speak of poems
or engage them in your
conference perhaps you feel
a tingle of recognition
of some sense that means
these words may reach
inside you and rest at
last in that place you
reserve for special spirits

Mouthfuls of Air

Say   I take a mouthful
of air and then squeeze
it out by words I speak
aloud begging them
to line up in an order
some sense of presence

Say   I describe how
I feel when I hear
a bird chirp after
a storm or I see
squirrels in a frantic
search for nuts or
I watch the fire catch
and send out heat
to my old cold bones

Say   I watch you dress
in the morning when
you think I'm sleeping
and my breath comes
in and out as easily
as tides flow in and out

Say   I tell you that
this air as it moves
in and out of my mouth
is not so much about breathing

Black Iris

I write as you sketch
        black iris
you set up your pad
select your pencil
and I watch your movements
your hands, your face
nothing dares to move
as you gather your perspective

The iris stirred by the breeze
challenges the authority
of an artist who will take
from it a moment
of its life

The lines of my verse
try to capture your
vision, write what you see
It shouldn't be hard
to draw into words
what you draw onto
        paper

But it is to me
I cannot outline the
petals by phrases
that may miss some
subtle stroke you make
some filling in of space
that creates that dark
flower which you will
make perfect for me

Continued

I try to make a phrase
perfect for you
but my black type
is a weak impression
for what I will see
when you finish
        for now   there is this lingering fragrance

Why I Write

Why Poetry Matters

Do I write lines
on paper as if
I were chiseling lines
on a cell's concrete wall?
               Last words?
Pressing down hard, breaking nails,
will that make the words come?

Suppose I was on death row.
What words would
I choose to leave?
Would I piece together
these lines which
the next prisoner
scrapes, leaving
every other one
paired with
her own words,
then to re-write the
words and lines
as hers?

My lines would
completely disappear
leaving no trace
that I was
               the one
who started this,
only now to end
with death
               my own
in this dark cell

in this corner
of my brain.
No remaining words.

I gave them all up
when I wrote
those first lines.

Words etched.
Scratched over.

Wiped off.

And if are not
selfishly taken, hoarded,

then they are simply
                gone.

If You Had a Working Number

Like the longitude
and latitude of
all the music
ever written
            ever sung
                        ever found

in your dreams
sounds came together
in one place
with the sun out
the clouds rare
the breeze slow

and all this made up
frets on an ebony
neck slim tight   tuned
to colors on
a hillside just
behind you
next to family farms
or just next to
any other land

all this waiting
for notes on an
airwave to pass by
settle on some
soft spot next to you

these are part of an
equation in progress
for the right number
      a line on a wine glass
           a line on a page
                a line on your hand
                      a line in a song

about why you were here
and why you spoke of
some desert that was
some dry barren place
and didn't mention
a word about how green
it was here
                or how it would all even out

Pristine Emptiness

In its chaste whiteness
lies a blank sheet of paper.
    Before the first word,
    before I put even a dash,
    before a line intrudes,

I sit here in emptiness.
In this hush, this silence
like a winter
snowfall I ponder

the perfection of
whiteness over everything.
The aristocracy.
The absoluteness.
A paper doesn't do anything
but reflect and wait for

words greater than anyone
can write– like
a shield held over
a wounded friend
who carves one word
in his own blood
before he shuts
his eyes and sleeps.

Wasting Metaphors

And how did this disease
this wasting metaphor to lost
causes seep into skin and bones
of those it came to serve
but not expecting to die

It's my verse that is the seat
of my torment   my angst
as I look for the perfect word
the perfect phrase to grab

See   I mean I'm swimming in
a marinade of my consciousness
            dark   thick   sweet   salty
            (the four tenets of poetry for me)

To pull them out of any other
context and push them into a
work of my own making could be
            rich   and   savory
as if it were this epic roast to
be braised for hours   maybe days
until every fiber within had yielded

And liberated the form   my electric
current   flowing in alternate directions
this magical ceramic tureen
where I could lift off the top
peer in and say

Stand by to be shocked

What We Seek

Asymmetry is
a plump wren perched
on a thin branch
contemplating
a ripe strawberry
stilled on a table

In its serene
pose does
the wren feel
ripeness or see
the redness or
is the setting
just a *pas de deux*
for one

Untangled

This poem I want to write
must be tight   the yarns
of verse threaded in so close
no light can sneak between the words

The verses must be a knot that
no one can untie   so it remains
this conciseness until a time
when this same poem

throws a tantrum to be loosened
and set free like a baby that
won't be held for one more minute
in swaddling clothes

All I have to do is
put the damn thing on paper
when I calm down
and we are both liberated

Digging in my heels
swearing that I can do this
makes me angry just enough
to punch out a good line

I hear worms laughing in my brain

Sand as Pearl

Imagine something that
is not quite right
it doesn't feel right
like a grain of sand
in a Chesapeake oyster

what if I put a word
in the middle of the page
and build a poem around it
layer upon layer with words
until a certain point
where it has a luster

and then I know
I could stop
anytime on my command
maybe the word
starting out wasn't
quite right–but
then by the time
I finish there
would be this pearl

first I have to
find this word
this right word
this not quite right right word

Blacksmoker

From a surface through zones
snow falls in magical ways
a field of red
darkness and pressure
the rawness of depths
blacksmoker belches
the hot and coldness
too extreme to touch
life exists at all edges
and forms layers
we cannot see
but we know much
is beyond the ordinary

Sine Qua Non

The poem of my life
is not yet written
I have more failures
to live through

the necessities of
poetic truth and
the pain from
lack of it

have yet to
reach me inside
where I can
crawl down
                where I must

dig deep into the
slush of my humanity
                where I must

see the disemboweled
the dismembered
the raw bones of those
who did not survive
the readings of other poets

when I finally see
all this and when I find
the poetic poise
to create lines
with words that
tell all who read
                my poetry

this is what
the truth is

then one will
look up and say
to the next one
        this poem actually works for me
                or something like that

I May Burn, But

My hot flash
is not the usual
singe of flesh
from within

Mine is the heat
of words which
smolder like
forgotten live coals
under a barely
smoking fire pit

The thought
of a breeze
won't cool my passion
but will bring flames
up from grey ashes

Ignite my eyes
to liberate the rush of tears
with each syllable
and tempt my mind
with each well-placed pause

To send me reeling
like I forgot that
water fuels a grease fire

Why I Drink

Early Morning

On a slow walk,
crisp air cleansed
from an overnight shower
leaves a grass blossom
with a single drop
of water hanging.

Its tip, held by
the concerted action
of atoms, stretches
for the ground,
tossing out electrons
until all the energy is
gone and the drop

must be released,
where it will disappear
into the ground,
atomic particles scattered.

Gravity of the
entire earth pulls
against that one drop;
and this same gravity

holds me earth-bound
lest I lift off and take
the drop with me to

save for some future thirst.

Aqua Vitae

An olive captured
in a martini glass
surfs small waves
(pity the olive–has to
swim or remain
pierced suspended
in clear waters)
drinkable only to a few

Before my lips consider
the glass's rim, before
my tongue engages
the crystal spirit
in that small solitary
moment, I see underneath
a freshwater lake–pure
waters held by miles
of frozen ice

Explorers worked for years
to find this pristine water
held, locked up,
submerged while I
on the surface can only dream
about waters of life
within an arm's reach

And as I part my lips
to take this first sip
I wonder
was I shaken or stirred...

Drinking a Secret

I have this secret
Frank Sinatra and I
share something
holding our liquor

When you ask me
do I want a cocktail
I say   *sure it's that time*
My lips pretend to purse
for a kiss but what
I really want is
to lick the verge
of that scotch lowball

What my fingers long
to stroke is the brow
on the perfect body
of a dry *verre á martini*

And when I shake
my raw truth
it's from pure anticipation

of holding my liquor
until I can't let go

Capote and Brando Talk Over Drinks

The bar is on the corner
of 5th and Nothing Else
they talk about
their favorite gins
and other booze
that killed their parents

But that's too droll
even by their standards
so they talk about
great movie lines
and miscast roles

Truman interrupts
an opinion of his beret
would be nice
he found it at a
Goodwill store

Marlon wonders
if his black sweater
makes him look fat
They laugh at themselves
order another drink

talk about the weather
in Kansas and other
foreign locations such
as the prairie
cold this time of year

Continued

Grasses bitter and dry
under flawed breezes
held by their opinions
but that's the gin talking
they must not get
too carried away
with scenes they
do not create

In all directions
they look around
hold their hands
up to frame
the outside–
fitting what they can
into the box

Between sips both
agree not much
is likely to change
their forecast

Irish Whiskey

Sitting at the bar
at the C & O
handsome rail it is
well-worn and thick
hickory (I think)

Whiskey choices
dazzle me
many bourbons
and ryes
with "creek"
        in their names

I pick the Bushmill's
feeling a bit Irish
like I'm lucky
        or something
through an open window
I hear the street
Clicks   scrapes   shuffles

Later at the bus station
waiting for
number ten
two young black men
they're messing around
calling each other *nigger*
tugging crotches in low pants

But there is just us
and I'm sitting here

Continued

thinking like I used to
about all those
unfamiliar   conferences
nameless   cities
wasted   minutes
waiting   waiting
wondering what in
the world
was I doing here

Black Pelican

On a roughed up sea
the hunt begins

Food in the form
of liberated infants
is just below the surface

And all the fowl
with their watering mouths wait
at the bar for just the right
moment to fill empty gullets

Half shells wash up during
the night and still glisten
with the emptiness left

After oysters and clams
have long gone to food
for others who have searched
and waited for the right spice

And in just a small moment
a tiny pearl was pushed
over to my hand
                    the hand that held the whiskey

Lifesavers

It's the wine at the new place
                    just outside of town.
The spring has ambled on in.
One day it is just here.
A Petit Verdot
falls asleep on my lips.
My tongue takes advantage.

People emerge like ground
bees sensing light for the
first time, testing air, testing
water, tasting wine.
All nibble the edge of a manchego,
decide to stay and see what develops.

Sips of Viognier slip
between the aches and pains, stiff
feet, knees, and little nuisances on faces.
Talk of slim prospects for writing
wedge between slices of smoked meats.

An asymmetrical cutting board
presents itself under a humble
organic turkey burger that does not come
certified, but does match well
with a nice rosé.

At the end, talk concludes among travel
postcards of Chicago, the Outer Banks, a
cabin in Colorado, buried still in snow.
But the dog, whose eyes are stitched shut,
does not care.
He noses a familiar hand for a treat.

Searches in other pockets only yield
a lifesaver, stuck to an old
band-aid, between the *Rs* and the *Ss*
in an address book.

And was it you who asked if anyone had a mint
before leaving?

Beach Glass

If you find
a large piece
of beach glass
            rub your fingers
                    over it
                            repeatedly.
Look closer at
the frosted texture
fixate on its origin
            what roughed it smooth.

Make up a good story
about how it came
to be in your hand,

Perhaps a wine carafe
thrown into the surf
a celebration
            or a funeral.

No, better yet
a scorned lover
did not forgive
            much less forget.

And now this
weathered shard
a periclase anomaly
has appeared
            in your hand.

A gift for you,
a new creation
comes forth.

The story comes alive.
Touch the glass again.
Ah, yes, you can
                see it now:

                        She waited too long
                        the chardonnay had turned.

"... that is not stone
and turns no one to stone
who really stays to see her."
– **Sandra McPherson**

Just This Once

Outer Space

"...feel the future dissolve in a moment,
like salt in a weakened broth."
–Naomi Shihab Nye

I float out of
my window to
tunes of lawnmowers
cutting grass
blowing dust
against neighbor's beans and peas

As I hover above,
held in this space
by waves of sound
    and the breeze,
I feel so much

This summer—
so far it's good
and I feel like
writing a poem

I have to see
something first
I have to grab a thought
to start the pen
that's when I
see leaves move
    the dust flies
the sounds carry
the scratches on paper

And I conspire
with all this
to find a line
a good line
a life line
           My future came
                   from some brine
                         a long time ago

Marshall Ave. Winter 1954

On a front porch
as cold a winter
as can be remembered
the lid of the milk jar
has risen two inches
on now frozen cream

The cat, as black as
the cream is white
prowls over takes
a tentative lick
and licks again

Breakfast is hurried
inside   coffee brews
adults all take cream
child hears a scratch
no one moves to the door
but then there is the cat
        this pink tongue
                this black cat
                        this white cream

Marshall Ave. Spring 1954

Mock orange starts its
annual spray of fragrance
bulbs have sent their blossom
messengers up out of the dirt

A young girl jumps on
her pogo stick
              bomp   bomp   bomp
on the sidewalk of her world

A cat stands guard
at a new hole near
the big tulip poplar
sniffs the air and remains still

And an old woman
peers out her dining room
window   watches the girl
      and wrings her hands

              bomp   bomp   bomp

Marshall Ave. Summer 1954

The scents of all that surround
both houses lift upward
rising on the remains of heated
thermals escaping the
arrival of night air

As they give way they bring
the aromas of some things
sweet   a bourbon   perhaps
a berry pie   or the daintiness
of *Diamond Jubilee* rose petals

All these rise in the
cooling air having secured
free safe passage
through a window
to find rest on the head

Of a sleeping girl
who nods in agreement

Marshall Ave. Fall 1954

Grass and leaves crackle
for the first time
the little girl kneels   picks
at acorns and dried mulberries
her jacket is now a little small
for her   the jeans just a little short
knees a little worn   but
her cap is plenty big over black
curly hair that reflects a little
of the fall sun
and by the Chinese elm the
cat sees its breath   looks at
an old nest   licks a paw

In the distance against a
cold blue sky   scant of clouds
smoke rises from a chimney
higher
            and still higher

Sometimes the Norfolk & Western

what if   you saw
this train   it passes through
this half-done   town on its way
to bigger   plans and you
stood still   but this minute
movement   you had was
due only   to the earth
going about   its business
the train   would move
away at   two speeds
earth's   and its own

and there   was this
person on   board who
saw you   and thought
about how   some things
appear to   stand still
yet also   fade away

The Weightiness of Dreams

I've put my dreams
on this paper
now I can't
get them back
I want to know
what the dreams
meant

    The one where
    my father sits
    in a chair in his
    dark store
    and does crosswords
    with a pen that
    doesn't write

    The one where
    my mother knits
    holes in her fingers
    but doesn't bleed
    on yarn that doesn't end

    The one where
    I look for them
    but I'm told
    I just missed
    the door closing
    behind me

I take a knife
and try to pry
the words up but
it's no use
the gravity won't let go

Indigo

I need an indigo cavern—
a colossal, odoriferous
pain-swelling blackness.

It has to take me
to a shore where I can
feel a slime, an extravagant

mucous, from inside
of my heart which
has fallen on a rusted nail.

This slow tearing—
fiber by fiber pulls
the blood out to
run along my hand.

My white, blue-veined
gnarled appendage
pushes the nail

deeper and deeper
until I feel it come
out of the other side

of this tiny worm hole of a poem.

Voices

I hear voices
mingled families
here and past
they rise and fall
among the redbuds
through the jonquils
return to the porch
where they settle in
among the chairs
on the sleeves of my sweater

breaths I mistake
for breezes flow
through windows
across countertops
and like rafts on
a flat lake
float among my thoughts

when I   talk
of my past
and when I   listen
for hints of yours
I hear these voices
these young sounds
that will fly
into the air
twirl in their
own dance   sing
of their brevity
and disappear

Obscure Virginia Reels

Lonely holler girl
waits her fate in jail
                again
after another
Saturday night

in a down and out
little country town
where nothing happens
                good   or   bad

Traveling evangelists
set up tents next door
in stale cow pastures
where crowds come round
plaid dresses mix with dungarees

To hear some different news
                some good   some bad

Cars pass by while
shiny pick-ups plow
across broken grass
and unload a few
to hear the good word

Streets now empty
dried up in summer night,
take no notice of lovers
as they "do-si-do"
at the regular VFW dance.

Bad words get in the way.
Some drink a little much
and the next day all will
be forgiven, but not for
ones who crossed over
the line, not the salvation
line, it's the other one,

the one where you forgot
who you fought and why.
Then you landed your sorry
ass in jail where you listened
to that country holler girl
wail as she did this stupid
two-step to a ratty bunk bed.

Deep Water Behind the Store

On many Sunday mornings
with my father
working his books
I could hear her wails

Whispers and pleadings
pouring like cheap whiskey
came out of the jail

Saturday night's drunken
fun left unpleasant
remnants not
especially kind
or considerate
in those circumstances
where

a few bruises here and there
from many stumbles
on street curbs
were not mistaken
for any badges
of honor

There were no greetings
or requests for encores
and I was told
to ignore the sounds

But I would hear her laments
look at my father
who would frown

and go back to his
bookkeeping on
the counter
in front of his miniature
whiskey collection

I found it hard to
read my grammar books
where words fell flat
So I switched to
Endangered Fishes of Virginia

I liked the pictures
of the big ones landed
on shore with the
men standing around
smiling at their prize catches
their hands cupping small
glasses of dark liquid

Fog Rises and Sets

Through a frosted window
I could not see the cold

But felt it inside my bones
The distant water was warm

The rising fog
Lifted off a stilled pond

Drifted through stagnant fields
To a wood chilled

Crossed an old wash
Where it hovered

Then reversed
Drawn back to the pond

To start the rising
All over again

Still the mist moved
Up and toward the woods

Where at last it disappeared
Yet I watched such flights

I knew not the time nor
Whether to stay or flee

Just This Once, Another Once

1

I look backward through a storm
raging dark with lightning stabbing
trees into submission
flashes outside
mirror flashes inside
my head with all
that I remember
from a childhood so
very long ago yet
burns inside without
any resolution or
attempt to quench

Just once, another
once can bring out purple threads
that sew up my eyes

It is my life I see
from the growing up
parts from my youth
at the store
at the house
at the farm
of my mother's sister
where I faced cousins
who seemed as strangers
to me but somehow
loved like we belonged
and the farm animals

Continued...

had the same connection
I first felt the teat
of the milk cow and
the flesh felt familiar
not strange and
milk came forth
when I squeezed
hot steaming into
a dented bucket
and later would
be poured into the churn

This same sister many
years later would arrive
at our house and
greet me with sighs
and sadness of one
who knows she has
little time left to
live and must see
her siblings one more
time and when my
mother cried   I cried too

O, the sourness
from clabber before sweetness
of cold churned butter

I feel lost connections
from my parents when
I return to look at the house
my noble father
who could withhold
secrets and
who lived on an island
where his only

company was his camera
My mother as a paradox
who in frustrated
domestication
found her conflicts
with child rearing
and fierce independence
created a malaise
which she fought
for years to overcome

Even across the abyss
that was the hallway
in our home
where my room
opposite my father's
was too close
I heard the
pleadings from him
to her as
she walked on
to her bedroom about
a thousand miles
from ours
her refusal of
intimacy made for
an intolerable marriage
filled with conditions that

A youngster would never
understand but would always
despair at her ignorance
of those adult ways
which forced their
malaise into walls

Continued...

and woodwork and
creaking of beds made
soundless of doors
closing and lights extinguished

I saw out the windows
of this house and
wished for far off places
where I could be safe
and I could feel
the universe all around
with answers waiting
for me to discover
but within my youth
the limits of the town
were barriers stronger
than prison wire
and when I found a way
to break through
the exit was not
pretty but was
the right thing to do

2

I see the house
at once dark and at another once
lit up as if spotlights
have been thrown out of the sky
on it from every direction
all the buried boards
bones unearthed
exposed as if to be counted

and fought over
like currency gathered
for a big purchase
but will not happen
for this house
is not for sale

It is the house where I grew up
and now I see through
the wrong end of a telescope
tiny receding figures
getting farther and farther away
at once and then another once

The home is huge and lonely looking
windows are closed eyelids
all the light is on the outside
nothing comes from within

And the rooms inside
have their native darkness
spelled by certain
leavings with only
things going out and
little coming in

The streets are dark   wet
and I cannot walk in any direction
my feet are heavy and sodden
stuck in a dark path
I should know but can't find
I stand and stare with the town
                              behind me
I cannot turn away and
look at anything else

Continued...

But I return to
the store drawn into
an orange glow
a light that is not bright
or familiar   I
look around and there
is no one I recognize
I head up stairs
and see someone
behind a counter
I ask where is everyone
and she replies
they are all gone
but where is Mr. Robinson
and she replies
he's somewhere around
and I say
I write poetry
she makes no expression
I turn to go
back down the stairs
I do not find him
when I return
to the street
it is dark
I walk toward the
railroad tracks which
I must cross
before I can see my house
or whatever may
be living within

3

Another once shows the trees
in a green summer stage
a season from my youth
or my adulthood
or in my old age
but that is the only color I see

There is this coldness
rising above the house
hanging in the air
like it is waiting for someone
to grab it and
confine it in some lidded
box rather than some tomb

This once I hear something and
then another once the sound
seems very far off
ghostly voices fade
amidst the rain
I stretch toward sounds
but the whispers are
too faint   too soft
too gone

Whispers drifted into ether
that is the universal space
where they will be
lost among the millions
of other whispers
where my mortal self

Continued...

cannot tell them apart
from any others
and what I must do
is wait until I
can follow my own
whispers into this cosmos
to settle in a void
where I will be content

I find the high walls
of barren rock
some covered with snow pack
speak to me of a
durable surface
some roughness amidst
the coldness that shouldn't
be comforting to me
but strangely is

The solidarity of dark
surfaces rising from
ground covered in
softness is similar
to my home which rose
from a stone foundation

And withstood the
shakes and tremors of
multiple quakes and
landslides that most
would like to forget
but come back to me
as sequences or episodes
of when I met with
old friends in unfamiliar

shapes and voices
Who spoke to me
of how I could love them
and possibly forgive them
for all they said or might
have done   or had not
I wondered if they
meant my mother
or my father and
whatever unfinished business
we take with us
when we realize
now we are old and
must resolve any
internal conflicts remaining
so we can uncover
not just some

Sorrow or remorse
but we can regain
something that we lost
or we can retake some
measure of what we can love
and how we know we could
not have imagined any losses

At that time
I could not believe
little future regrets
or missed opportunities
would come to me
at those moments
when I had to take
them both off life support
not ever knowing what would

Continued...

have happened if I
had not let them go
In advance of my
sleep every night
I wonder what scene will
come to me as I
drift off in final moments
sometimes I am here
sometimes I am where
I know nothing of the
people and place
but it all is familiar
dark   somber
the people speak
slowly and move
with deliberation

4

I remember names
of friends from so long
ago I cannot remember
why I knew them
or where I knew them
but I find them
we speak but
we don't talk

Just like cousins
from whom I am many
times removed by
state of mind more
than state of blood
I cannot help
them and they

cannot find me
We are in parallel
worlds made by paths
laid on different tracks
we travel on
and on into our
own times with
our own baggage
packed with whatever we
know we cannot live without

For me all
I know is to write this
as if it is the last poem
I'll ever compose

Just once, another
once can bring out ruby threads
sewn into my words

I have dreamt all this
once and then another once

Temperate Zones

I am not just one person.
It is quite difficult to
simply be myself. I
must explode in
different temperature
zones to show you
all the ways I can
be—and still be
a form of myself.

I have formed
as if through
ages of ice, fire,
and stone only
to come now
in the grip of
an age. One in
which I can talk
about how I
came to be
a woman, a poet,
some sense of
oneness with others.

Couldn't I simply
have been formed
by clay and water
in a universal mold
where I would have
fit just as well as
everyone?

But where then
would have been
the age of light
for me? Something
that would have
sparked the one
thing I found.
It has been no
easy task to
simply find myself.
After all, there
are so many others
whose parts I coveted.

Another Poem About Time

Driving home between
mountains and the long stretch
in front of Merck where the
boys used to race,

I see my home
every time I cut off
onto back roads.

I see our store and I know my
father is waiting on some customer
who can't decide between boots,
shoes, or not spending at all.
Both desperate in their silence.

I see my mother in the house
on Spotswood where she's
sitting in the dim living room
with her little TV, fiddling
with worn-out letters in
her Boggle game.

I'm still heading home
but the road
gets harder and the car won't
move, so I get out and walk
thinking I'll go faster. But

I don't get any closer and now
the time is past and when someone
asks why don't people talk about
time anymore I think I know
           what they mean.

There is this notion that if I don't find just the right stone, this smooth, electric piece of the earth, with its consolidation and complexity, I won't be able to find the right words either. But that is just a lie I tell myself to keep writing.

Sara Robinson, July 2013

www.ingramcontent.com/pod-product-compliance
Lightning Source LLC
La Vergne TN
LVHW041306080426
835510LV00009B/884